MEET THE MONKEY!

Written by Keith Faulkner
Illustrated by Robert Morton

GT PUBLISHING

Copyright © 1996 Brainwaves Limited.
All rights reserved. No part of this book may be used or reproduced
in any manner whatsoever without written permission from the publisher.

This edition published by GT Publishing Corporation.

For information address GT Publishing Corporation, 16 East 40th Street,
New York, New York 10016.

ISBN: 1-57719-093-9

Printed in Singapore.

Meet the Monkey

Monkeys are members of the primate family. They are classified into two groups. Old World monkeys come from Africa, Asia, and the Far East. New World monkeys come from Central and South America. The chart below shows you some of the other primates. Let's take a closer look at one of the most acrobatic of the New World monkeys—the spider monkey.

man

apes

Old World monkeys

marmosets

New World monkeys

tarsiers

aye-ayes

indrises

lemurs

tree shr

The spider monkey lives in the trees in the rain forests of Central and South America.

The Face

The spider monkey has large eyes located in the front of the head. This enables it to have good vision, which is important for leaping through the treetops. The spider monkey's ears are small and often hidden by fur. Like humans, spider monkeys use their expressions to communicate with each other.

 Turn to the back of the book and press out the head piece.

"Fear": upper teeth exposed

"Playfulness": mouth open, but upper teeth covered

"Excitement": lips pursed

The Torso

To live in the treetops, a spider monkey needs a strong, lightweight body. Like all mammals, the spider monkey's torso is covered with warm fur. The fur keeps the monkey and its young warm.

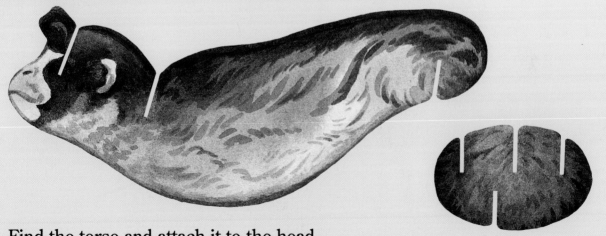

Find the torso and attach it to the head.

The Legs

The spider monkey has long, slender legs, and feet that can grip as well as its hands. Each foot has a big toe that works like a human thumb and can be used to grasp branches. The spider monkey's legs act like powerful springs for leaping huge distances from branch to branch.

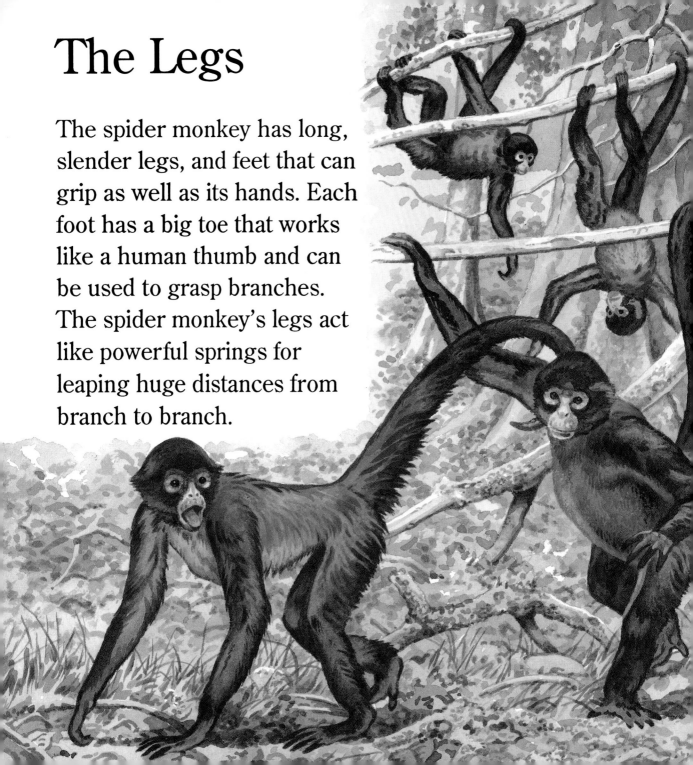

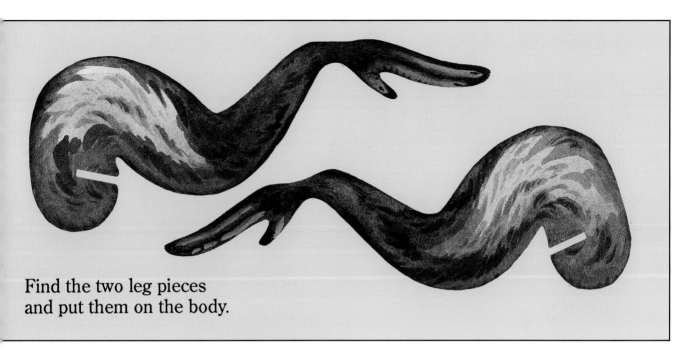

Find the two leg pieces
and put them on the body.

The spider monkey
rarely leaves the safety
of the trees, but it can
walk upright for short
distances. It uses its
long arms and tail
for balance.

The Tail

The spider monkey has a long, strong, and flexible tail with a pad of bare skin under the tip. Its tail helps the spider monkey to balance when it is climbing and leaping in the trees. The spider monkey can also use its tail as a fifth limb for holding food while it eats.

The tail grips branches so firmly that the spider monkey can hang by its tail alone.

Now find the monkey's tail and attach it to the torso.

The Arms

The spider monkey's arms are very long and slender. Unlike most monkeys, the spider monkey has no thumbs. To swing through the trees, the spider monkey hooks its hands on branch after branch. Its hands are also used for climbing, feeding, and grooming.